Are You Listening Now?

Are You Listening Now?

DORSET AND SOMERSET YOUNG PEOPLE 2024

StoryTerrace

Text Paddy Magrane, on behalf of StoryTerrace
Copyright © Future Roots

Text is private and confidential

First print July 2024

StoryTerrace

www.StoryTerrace.com

CONTENTS

FOREWORD FROM THE LORD LIEUTENANT OF DORSET	7
CHAPTER 1: JACK'S STORY	15
CHAPTER 2: REECE'S STORY	21
CHAPTER 3: LUCY'S STORY	29
CHAPTER 4: CHARLIE'S STORY	35
LIFE ON THE FARM	41
CHAPTER 5: JORDAN'S STORY	53
CHAPTER 6: CHLOE'S STORY	57
CHAPTER 7: VEE'S STORY	63
CHAPTER 8: ABI'S STORY	69
CONCLUSION	75
EPILOGUE: HARVESTING HOPE	83

FOREWORD FROM THE LORD LIEUTENANT OF DORSET

I first met Julie Plumley at an annual general meeting for Dorset Community Foundation where she was giving a talk about Future Roots at Rylands Farm and the work she was doing there. That talk was about the Countrymen initiative, which brings retired countrymen such as farmers and gamekeepers together to combat the isolation and loneliness that can ensue once such men are confined indoors —something that is the complete opposite of their former lived experience. It was only later that I was lucky enough to be introduced to the work that Julie and her team were doing to support young people through her care farm. This location combines the outdoor farming environment, including animal therapy, and the calming effect of working outdoors with education and care. In short, using the natural cycle of working outdoors to settle young individuals into a trusting and constructive frame of mind—a positive re-set to their outlook on life and work.

This book looks at the challenges that some young people, particularly those who find themselves at the more extreme end of life's difficulties, have to tackle, as they see them through their own eyes. The title and the theme of the book *Are You Listening To Me Now?* refers to a deeper kind of 'listening' than is often applied in language. Through the thoughts put into words by a number of the troubled young people that Future Roots at Rylands Farm has helped in the past, this book illustrates the true meaning, the code if you like, of what they are struggling with in their own lives and why their environment has failed them. It is a clue as to why the young should never be abandoned as a lost cause. I feel so lucky to have been born into a loving, secure and stable environment which has enabled my life chances and opportunities. Many of us take our lives for granted and take little time to recognise the wasted lives of those whose environment has trapped them, both mentally and physically, into a dead-end of rejection and violence, victims of fear and circumstance. These accounts of the thoughts of young people enable us to see more clearly what the message is behind the words and actions of those who are the victims of extreme circumstances. They should enable us to decipher the needs below the surface of these difficult lives and, hopefully, be able to recognise what they really mean and how to meet those needs and improve the life chances of these victims of circumstance and misunderstanding.

It is all too easy to write off those that appear to be causing trouble, to exclude them from the normal run of education and development as 'disruptive.' They can be extremely disruptive, but this book illustrates that, in so many cases, these lives can be turned around. Through understanding and a caring environment, they can become useful and fulfilled citizens. It does require us to 'listen' to the real message behind their behaviour. Such young people can appear frightening and out of control. If not 'rescued,' they are vulnerable to the malign influences of criminal adults and can easily be used as participants in crime through such influences.

A number of years ago, I was privileged to meet a young man who features in this book. His name was Reece and although, I believe, about 16 years old, he was an extremely big youngster. So much so, that the two young male carers who were working with him at the time looked small. He appeared calm, happy and absorbed in the task they were working on. In fact, other than his size, it was a normal scene of pleasant interaction. I learned a little of his story later and was astounded to learn of the home, school and general educational difficulties that he had experienced and the malign influences that had taken advantage of his rejection by, and ejection from, any interpretation of a normal young person's life. I learned how he had been rescued through the influence and environment of Future Roots as Rylands Farm and had come to love his visits. He had found a trusting and caring environment and he found it easy, within that, to be caring and positive himself. The contrast between his life, the 'gang culture' that he had been sucked into outside Ryland's, was extreme, but he appeared to be trying very hard to break away from his old ways. He did, at one point, cease to attend the farm as his 'mates,' as he called them, tried to break his attachment with the farm, but, on that occasion, the Rylands team managed to find him and bring him back to regular attendance. Unfortunately, Reece was, in the end, persuaded by his 'mates' to return to his old life and his life was ended by a drug overdose. Although Reece's story does end in tragedy, it also illustrates that a vulnerable individual, who had been lost to society through criminal influence, could be saved through a trusting and caring environment. Unfortunately, in Reece's case, the claws of his malign 'mates' had been driven into his young life too deeply and, in the end, he found it impossible to break away. This shows how a safe and caring natural space can help a lost soul improve and create the chance for a changed life. It also illustrates the need to act early in such extreme cases to try to break the pattern before it is too late, as it was in Reece's case.

The work of Rylands Farm, working with animals and nature and an atmosphere of mutual trust, has been proven to be an extremely positive influence and it enables many young people who are severely challenged by the circumstances of their lives to positively re-set their lives and improve their future. As the title of this book implies, we need to listen to them and learn how to listen to the real message behind their words and actions. The biggest challenges in the lives of these young people tend to be within four main areas. These are not exclusive but are the main areas of issue: they are problems within the school environment, within the area of mental health, the problems that can emerge from relationships and the stretched support services that are trying to support them notwithstanding the shrinking resources available to take this challenging job on. For a few from disadvantaged homes, school can be extremely challenging as the young can be picked on over 'differences.' This destroys their self-respect and confidence. Mental health, both within the youngsters themselves and also, on occasion, within the family, is a big challenge and again can be a target for peer rejection if not handled sensitively. This is not always a simple task within the school environment. Relationships both within the home and at school can cause individuals to feel isolated and a target, particularly in the modern world of constant electronic communication. Those whose task it is to try to 'rescue' the young people at the extreme end of these difficulties have a hugely difficult task to fulfil; I see this book as a path to decipher the messages that these young people, whose stories are within these pages, are trying to get across to us, showing a way of translating the causes of their difficulty and opening up an opportunity to understand their plight and find a better pathway to helping them move their lives forward positively.

What comes out of these individual stories for me is the need for trust and patience with these young and troubled people. This enables an atmosphere of mutual respect in a very changed and natural environment that is the farm—a positive break from their normal experience.

What is being done by Julie and her team at Future Roots at Rylands Farm is quite remarkable and I see this book as an inspired way to break new ground in getting an even better understanding of the problems these young people face. This, in turn, should lead the way to further evolve the support available to them.

I have found that the young people's words and thoughts in this book have increased the depth of my understanding of their plight and a possible pathway out of their difficulties. I do hope that it does the same for you.

Angus Campbell

Angus Campbell.

Future Roots Awards Evening – celebrating opportunities for young people.

CHAPTER 1: JACK'S STORY

My name's Jack, and I'm 20 years old. In contrast to a lot of kids who find their way to Future Roots at Rylands Farm, I had a good childhood, at least at the start. My family was a happy one, and I loved my primary school, where I had lots of friends and enjoyed learning and after-school clubs.

But then I left my little village school and started at my secondary school in Sherborne. I'm not great with change and it was a massive shock to the system. But it wasn't just the shift that affected me. I was quite a big child for my age and you know what teenagers are like—they always pick on anyone who's different, and they turned on me because of my weight.

The school didn't do much to tackle it. There was one lovely teacher, Miss Voytovich, who tried to help, but then she went on maternity leave and decided not to come back, so I was left to fend for myself.

The bullying was hard enough, but there was also the environment. I'm diagnosed with Asperger's and struggled in the much larger classes. I received a bit of support from a one-to-one assistant, who helped me do my work, but it wasn't enough, and I became increasingly stressed in the classroom.

In time, I was spending most of my day in what the school called 'the blue room,' which was a quiet space with computers for kids who, like me, found the classrooms tough. I was on my own in that room a great deal, and after a while I realised I wasn't really at school, at least not in a meaningful way. I was just catching up on homework, or else sitting there fiddling with my phone, which felt like a sort of internal exclusion.

By the start of Year 8, I was struggling to attend. I couldn't motivate myself to go when I knew a day of being distracted or bullied in the classroom, or loneliness in the blue room, lay ahead of me. That was when my parents heard about Future Roots at Rylands Farm. There were a handful of older kids at The Gryphon who came to the farm, and it was suggested that I try it out too.

At first, I was very wary. I knew of the kids who attended and wasn't keen to spend time with them.

To begin with, I came one day a week. I remember those initial visits. It was all so new to me—a farm, instead of a traditional school—and I was really scared at first.

But within a few months, I knew it was going to be OK. The staff were really friendly and welcoming, and I realised that, rather than being a threat, the kids from my secondary school were in the same boat as me. They weren't necessarily being bullied, but they had something going on—some problem they were dealing with—and it changed my perspective.

Once I'd settled here, Dorset County Council arranged for me to attend Future Roots four days a week (on the other day, I did odd jobs).

ARE YOU LISTENING NOW?

I absolutely loved it here and was soon immersed in all the jobs that need doing on a farm—working with the cows, feeding the animals, clearing out the horses' stable and exercising them (although to be honest, I avoided that bit as I'm not keen on horses!). In between, there was lots of fun, spending time in the fresh air—going on walks by the river, for instance. In contrast to school, we were never stuck in a classroom. It was where I wanted to be, and my parents could see that I was happier.

I also took two land-based City & Guilds certificates here, qualifications that are linked to Kingston Maurward College. Even though I was studying, the staff here weren't like teachers. They were friendly and relaxed, and never took themselves too seriously. They also showed us students respect, and that meant we gave it back.

If I had a problem at secondary school, the solution was to chuck me in the blue room on my own. If I had a problem at the farm, I found a member of staff or Julie. But the thing was, I rarely had any big problems, because I felt calm and happy here.

The staff here really worked to support me at my pace, and with a style of learning that worked for all of us. Obviously, there were lots of practical tasks and I learned by actually doing. But when there was something academic to be tackled, we all approached tasks based on our capacity. Say there was a bit of work that involved five questions. If you could only manage two that day, you only did two. Or you did two, went outside to do some farming work, then came back in refreshed to attempt some more.

It sounds like there was no time frame, and that would be wrong. There was always an overview of what we needed to achieve, but never that stressful sense of homework that had to be completed by the next day.

There was also a chance to talk through work and assignments as a group. That's been one of the best things about this place—the sense of family and community, of approaching things together. And if you wanted individual help, there was always a staff member with whom you could have a chat.

It's meant that I've achieved what I needed to without the stress of an examination when my mind always used to go blank.

Being here allowed me to learn my own way, but also to discover my passion, which is farming. It's in the blood, I think. Dad and Grandad had both worked on farms, Grandad since he was 12 years old.

These days, I work self-employed on a dairy farm. I spend my days milking and scraping up, which involves using a tractor to clean up the shit the cows leave behind. After that, I'm busy bedding, laying chopped straw down for the cows.

I started off with one day a week and built my hours up slowly. I began with a big dairy farmer around here, and now I'm with a smaller outfit.

I'm happy these days. In fact, I don't think I've ever been happier.

I've just finished a seven-week herdsman course with the vets, which covers all aspects of dairy farming. In time, I'd like to be a dairy farmer, maybe take on the lease of a farm so I'm running it myself.

Looking back, I wish I'd not been forced at school to learn subjects that never interested me, in an environment that I found really stressful. I realise it's not simple. In a school the size of my secondary, you can't individualise everything. But in an ideal world, it would be great to tailor learning a little to the child. Because if we're passionate about the subjects we're being taught, we're going to do so much better.

If I had been listened to earlier at school they would have known I wanted to learn and wasn't being difficult; it was just really difficult to cope in that school. I needed a different sort of learning and space to do well. They did listen eventually but not before I became stressed and anxious. I also think that isolating kids, as I was in the blue room, isn't the solution to crowded classrooms. It was like a punishment, which made me feel like an inconvenience.

I was lucky to find Future Roots. It gave me the boost I so desperately needed. And in the long term, true confidence.

I dedicate my story to Future Roots, for listening to me when I needed it the most.

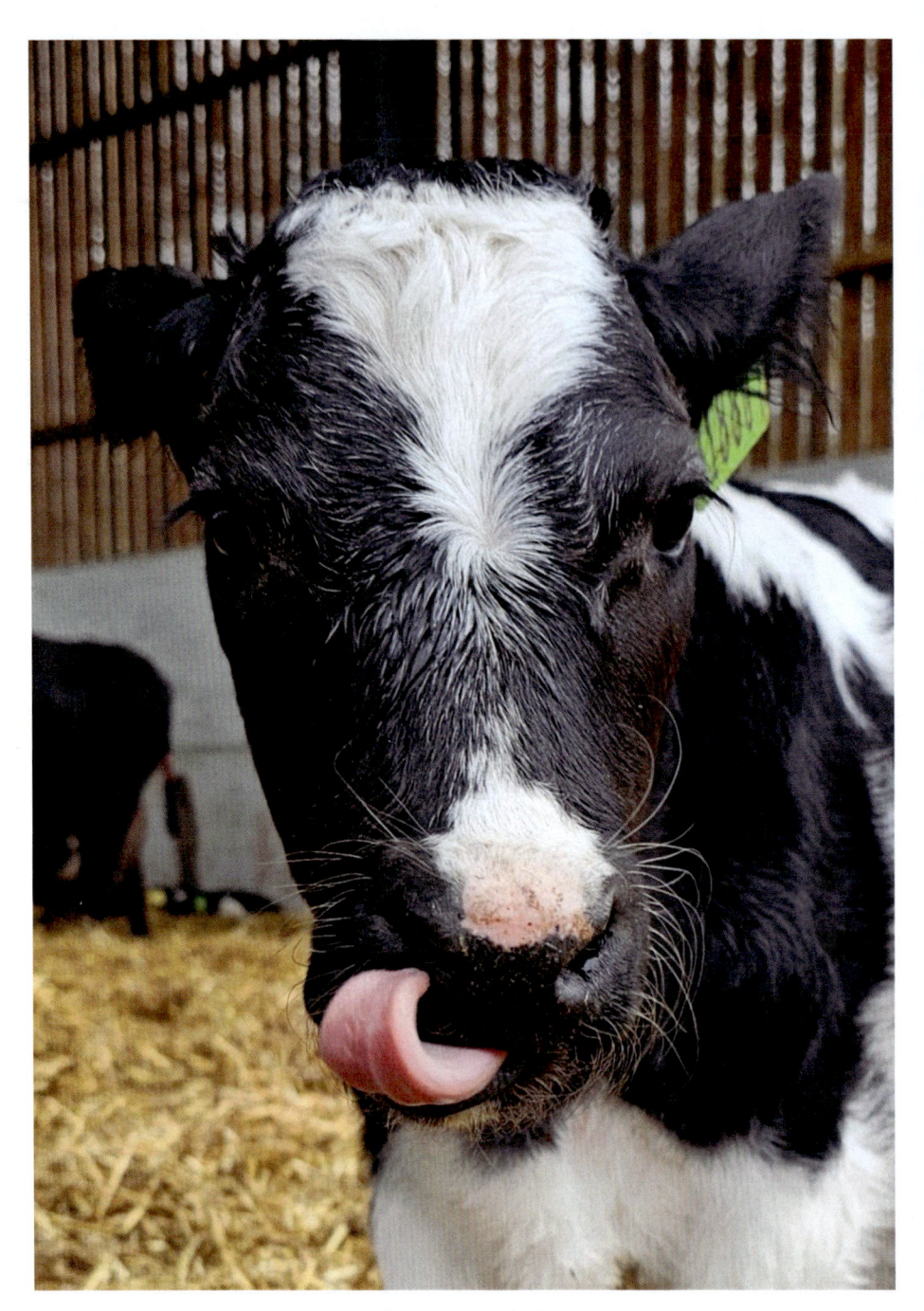

The cleanest nose in Dorset.

CHAPTER 2: REECE'S STORY

Reece tragically died on 3rd July 2018, a month before his 17th birthday. We have told his story in words we believe he would have used himself.

When I was young, my stepdad was away a lot, so it was just me and Mum. I remember it as a happy time, when we laughed a lot. Primary school was OK. I was bigger than most of the kids in my class and I was pretty good at sport, but it never really felt like my classmates were happy when I won. I had one good friend I used to spend time with out of school, but in school, there was some name-calling. I never really took any notice back then.

In middle school, the name-calling got much worse. I was still bigger than most of the other kids and had a very round head, which they all made reference to. I started to feel like I was ugly. I got really upset about it but I don't think I ever told anyone. I felt somehow like I needed to cope on my own.

I stopped playing sports because the teachers and other children used to say I was too rough. Truth was, I was just bigger than my classmates and a bit clumsy.

ARE YOU LISTENING NOW?

One day I hit another boy who was calling me names and saying things about my mum. I didn't realise how hard I had hit him, and I got excluded and sent to a learning centre.

My life suddenly changed. It was a scary place. All the lads were noisy and horrible to the teachers. None of them did as they were told. It was really shocking.

The staff asked me if I wanted to go to a farm and I jumped at the chance as I love animals. I went for two hours a week and gradually began to trust the team and other people on site. I loved playing team games and being useful and felt like I could be me at the farm—still hated writing though!

All I ever wanted was a dog, for my dad to want me and to be a policeman because I believe in fairness. I thought my size would be good for that career. I began to think that I could make things happen and that life was changing.

Back at home, my stepdad was around more. My relationship with him became really strained. I don't think we understood each other. He was sarcastic and it made me feel useless. I never felt good enough and he made me feel more stupid, which was also difficult for Mum. He wanted Mum's attention and I did too. I started to hang out more with the boys at the learning centre. It was just a laugh but I ended up getting more exclusions. I was offered two sessions at the farm of four hours, which was good, but often had a lot of time at home with nothing to do while Mum was at work. I hate being bored and on my own.

Occasionally I got told to rein in my language at the farm. I knew what was right and wrong but sometimes swore around adults or older lads because I thought it made me look tougher. I fed animals but we also played a lot of games and laughed. There were young people with learning difficulties and we made all sorts of games for them, which was fun. The adults at the farm made me do some writing but not loads. I was working to a qualification and although I hated writing, it felt good when I was helping out practically. I felt strong and helpful.

But at school, exclusions became more frequent. I used to punch walls a lot and there were more rows at home. I didn't really feel safe and it was easier to join in and be one of the lads there. A lot of them took drugs and talked like gangsters. They even shared the drugs at school.

I started spending time in Yeovil. I had family there and made 'friends' with lads a few years older. I also hoped I would see Dad around. I really hoped we would have a relationship. The mates I made didn't judge me. They did crazy, funny risky things that were a laugh. We climbed on roofs, drove cars, got drunk and smoked weed, running from police. They treated me like an equal and said I fit in really well with them. They introduced me to all sorts of experiences, and I thought it was exciting at first. But then it sometimes felt scary and as time went on, I witnessed some horrible violence. Then they encouraged me to nick my stepdad's car after we'd had an argument. That was the last straw at home and I got put into local authority care, although Mum didn't want me to go. It was only supposed to be for a short time. It should have been just a lesson.

I became angrier, confused, ashamed and sad. My 'mates' and the drugs helped me to forget when I was with them. I went to lots of homes but still messed about and started to learn the 'gang' ways, which scared lots of adults. They thought what I said was real. That I was bad. No one really liked me apart from the boys and the farm. I didn't mean what I said but no one really listened. People said I was a risk and I could see that few people trusted me. If I said something, they wouldn't bother to find out what was true and what was just an act. I lost a foster placement because I said I would kill their cat for muddy paws on my pillow. I would never have hurt an animal. It was just words. Other people say those things and no one worries. The farm knew that. They trusted me.

I had no one else but the farm a couple of times a week, and the lads, who were with me almost every night as well as some days. They told me not to bother with the farm, that it wasn't worth it. I stopped going for a few weeks when I lived with one of these friends out of county, but the farm came and found me. I mattered to them so I never stopped going again even when I was in care three hours away.

The farm listened and tried to help with my emotions but I needed more time. Every night, they called me to make sure I was safe. I hardly saw anyone else, most services only visited when there were reviews or something had gone wrong. There were changes of staff with every move of care home and all this time Mum was hoping things would change back to how they were. I saw some horrible things happen and did things I wasn't proud of, but my 'mates' told me I would always be bad like them and it was who I was.

ARE YOU LISTENING NOW?

As time went on, I believed what they said—that I was bad and would always be. Except when I had time at the farm. I was conflicted because I wasn't ever bad there. The boys said I could be the best, admired and feared. It sort of felt good. I would never hurt women, children or older people though. Whatever they said, I wouldn't do that. I protected the farm from them twice.

I became angry with all men. When I was mean or punched a man, it felt good, whoever they happened to be. I got a lot of praise for it from my 'mates' as well.

Every care home was another unsafe place. Far from the things and people that I felt comfortable with. Having to get on with other young people and fit in when I didn't feel like I did. My 'mates' always came to find me. Without them, I would have been painfully lonely. I did almost everything the boys said. I didn't have to, but I needed to prove I belonged and that I was part of them.

At the farm, I could still be a child and relax. I didn't have any responsibility. I only needed to keep safe and be kind. The pull of being with many of my 'mates' was less as time went by, but I had no one at all in the evenings. I was totally alone. I started to want Mum more. I started to plan for a change, but it was tough leaving the life with those boys behind. Some were real friends, I think, but they were all connected through the toxic lifestyle of drugs, drink and anti-social behaviour. They weren't all violent, but being friends with just a couple didn't work. It was all or nothing.

I needed more time. I would have found the way out, and what really mattered. But I trusted someone I called a friend even when I knew he was not trustworthy. I thought he would be OK with me.

Life ended too soon, and in a way that it shouldn't have.

If you had been listening, you would have heard how I felt when I was in middle school, hating the way I looked. You would have helped me with my self-esteem. You would have known I was protective over my mum because she was all I had, and you would have known I was clumsy. You would have known that I wanted to belong and would be easily led by others.

I needed a calm, safe space with positive role models early on. Maybe I should have been at the farm more than once a week. I did ask.

Later on, you would have known that what I was saying were just words used by my 'mates.' The stuff they had shown me, the violence, the rap. It wasn't really me. Many of them were not really my mates. I tried to let you know.

If you had heard me, you would have known the feelings of loneliness and despair that I felt in new placements. How unsafe I felt, the feeling of being trapped and that I couldn't get away easily from that lifestyle. It wasn't a choice.

I needed people who wouldn't give up on me. I didn't need to be placed in different counties, to have different workers. I couldn't cope with the change of people. I gave up talking to you.

If I was here, I would dedicate my story to Mum, Sam, Brian and Rachel because they never stopped believing in me and never gave up trying to help me come out the other side.

Conservation work – always having fun whilst working.

CHAPTER 3: LUCY'S STORY

My name's Lucy, and I'm 29 years old. My early childhood was OK, but life spiralled rapidly out of control at secondary school. It was there that I was bullied by two girls who had once been my closest friends. Teenage girls can be cruel but I never expected it from them. For reasons unknown I've never understood, they just decided to turn on me one day.

The bullying was 24/7—in school, at the riding stables where I loved to go on the weekends and in the holidays, and then on social media when I got home. We were all on an app called Bebo in those days, and they'd have a go on me there too, so there was literally no escaping them.

I felt so let down by the school, which hadn't addressed what was happening, and I began to refuse to go in. I didn't want to be where the bullying had happened—it was simply too traumatising—and eventually, I was sent somewhere else, to a place in Dorchester known as the 'school for misfits.'

It took me a few weeks and a lot of gentle persuasion from my parents to even attend, but I gradually started to realise that it wasn't going to be that bad. The school was based in an old vicarage, with a homely vibe and around four or five kids in the class. I learned so much better there, in an environment where I was able to concentrate and focus.

ARE YOU LISTENING NOW?

Every Friday, the school had what was known as an enrichment day, with various activities on offer, one of which was spending time at Future Roots at Rylands Farm. I'm a big animal lover, so without hesitation, I signed up.

On my first visit, I was so nervous I'd be bullied again that I asked my keyworker to come with me. I was a very shy, anxious, wouldn't-say-boo-to-a-ghost child. I was convinced I'd be picked on.

It was very different to how it is today—much more basic, with just a barn where all the social areas are now. That first day, the majority of the kids with me were from the 'school for misfits,' but most of them were older than me. My keyworker stayed all day, but as soon as I met Julie, who was so warm and welcoming, I knew I'd be safe at the farm.

When I left at the end of the day, I felt really great and I remember telling my mum all about it in a very excited voice!

Back in those days, the farm had cows, a couple of donkeys, goats, sheep, chickens, guinea pigs and rabbits. It's a difficult thing to explain, but animals helped me connect to humans. It was like they made it easier for me, breaking down barriers, if that makes sense!

In time, I made friends.

Me and Abi are really close now but I remember we hated each other at the start. Julie sensed we'd get on so she took us riding as she knew we both loved horses (even though Julie hates riding!). We bonded that day and haven't looked back since!

The farm very soon felt like a community, a place where we supported each other, and where I always felt heard.

Since then, I've had so many opportunities at the farm—chances I simply wouldn't have had if I'd not attended. I've studied for my City & Guilds in land-based qualification here. It has a mix of written and practical components and the staff here helped steer me through them all.

I was also able to take one of the farm's steers (male cows) to the Gillingham and Shaftesbury Show. Another student, Jake, was showing a cow and the two of us spent hours here halter-training the two animals so they could be led by the rein on the day. They had to be in immaculate condition for the show, so we needed to bathe and shampoo them to ensure their coats were glossy and spotless.

On the day, Sonya accompanied me, giving the steer a good nudge every now and then to get him to move, as he was a bit stubborn. Despite all our efforts, we came last! But we still got the rosette and it was an opportunity I wouldn't have missed for the world, and one I would never have had if I'd not been coming to the farm.

I came here every Friday while I was at school. When I moved up to agricultural college to study farming, it changed to a Wednesday, when I'd come in to help out with a group of kids. So now I was in a different position—a volunteer, but part of the team at the farm. It was a real step up for me. I felt trusted, validated. The staff saw I was capable and that I had potential.

Today, I have two kids of my own aged four and six. I'm also a domiciliary carer working with the elderly, which is an amazing job.

ARE YOU LISTENING NOW?

I still come in here, as the farm is very much an open house. Julie has always said I can drop in any time I like. I guess I'm part of the furniture here now!

If I've had a bad day and I'm feeling stressed, the farm makes me feel a lot better, particularly the comfort I get from spending time with the animals.

Looking back, I wish school had listened to me about the bullying—made me feel heard and seen. But instead, they actually put me in a room with the bullies. I guess it was their clumsy attempt to get us to sort out the problem between us. But it was totally traumatising. All I wanted was a chance to be listened to—to express how I felt, and how the bullying was affecting me.

So many schools get it wrong with kids. In my secondary school, I was dragged by my ankles across the foyer by a teacher. My mum had dropped me and I was so upset, and this was their solution—to literally force me into the school in the most cruel and humiliating way. That's no way to treat a child.

So yes, I'd say listen to children. You may not be able to solve all their problems, but being heard and understood is an incredibly powerful experience for a child when they're feeling lost or scared.

The other thing I'd encourage schools to do is help children who struggle to learn in the classroom. I'm the first to admit I have difficulty focusing. But at the farm, I've learned through practical tasks—by 'doing.' Give kids those chances, because it'll do wonders for their confidence.

My self-esteem soared at the farm. They saw me as a person, not a problem. This place is somewhere I can always turn to. My mum always says that I'm happier and more excited after I've visited. That's got to be a good thing!

I dedicate this story to Star, the Future Roots' beloved steer, who made such a difference in my life and who recently passed away.

Star – giver of confidence and love.

CHAPTER 4: CHARLIE'S STORY

My name's Charlie, and I'm 20 years old. It's fair to say my childhood wasn't a good one. My parents were both heroin users, more preoccupied with their drug habit than providing for me and my sisters. The house where we lived was an absolute shithole. In fact, it was so disgusting and filthy, that there were even mice scurrying across the floor. As a kid, I didn't really understand what clean or hygienic meant, but now, as an adult, I look back with horror. That house was truly appalling, the very worst place to bring up a child.

With drug addiction, there's a lot of chaos and unpredictability. When I was about six, my mum left. At the time, she was pregnant with my little sister. I was so innocent back then. I didn't really understand what was going on. I still don't, to be honest.

So at a stroke, it was me, my dad and my big sister (although she went to live with my grandad for a bit) left in the house.

One day my mother briefly returned in a terrible state with my little sister in her arms. It was nearly Christmas, and really cold, and there was my mum on the doorstep. She was wearing no shoes, and her face and arms were covered in bruises and cuts. I remember she told my dad that she had fallen off her bike, which obviously he didn't believe. There and then, she handed my little sister to Dad and walked away. We didn't see her for a few years.

My dad could no more look after my little sister than he could me, so I ended up raising her. She wouldn't even have eaten if I hadn't cooked us both meals. There's a YouTube video somewhere of me getting my sister ready for preschool, brushing her hair. I was only eight or nine years old, and what's known as a young carer, although I didn't realise it at the time. She's 13 now and we're so close.

Then, when I was about eight, my dad and I got kicked out of the house because he hadn't been paying the rent. We ended up living with my great-gran, but that was in a single room with a single bed together—me, my dad and my Staffy dog, Sasha.

I was old enough to know now that things weren't going well. There were visits from social workers, although I never saw much evidence of things changing. As an adult, I look back in disbelief that I was never taken into care. My hair was dirty and I never had a clean uniform or decent shoes for school. So why social services never took us into care is absolutely beyond me. I'd had a social worker before I was even born, so they knew all about the family.

I think I was like 12 when I first came to Future Roots at Rylands Farm. At the time, I was in a middle school in Dorchester. I'd not done that good in school up until that point.

I had always struggled to sit still and concentrate since and I've since been diagnosed with ADHD. My specialist says there's a hint of autism in there too, so that will also have been a factor in my childhood.

I think the school had heard about the farm and their thinking was that it would be a good fit for me, as I've always loved animals. I started attending one day a week.

I was a bit suspicious at first, as I would have been about going anywhere new, but when I turned up here, I actually realised that it was the best place for me. It felt, from the very start, like a safe place. In fact, I never wanted to go back to Dad. At home, there was chaos and no food, because he was shit at stuff like that. But at the farm, they'd cook for me—my favourite dish was scrambled eggs—and it felt like I was part of a family.

And of course, there were the animals!

I love the cows here. I think of all animals, they're amongst the most misunderstood. People tend to drive past cows in a field and just see a lot of black and white fat things chewing grass and looking a bit vacant. But once you get out there and meet them, you realise a herd contains some very distinct personalities. Take Jessie J at Rylands Farm, for instance. She's such an attention seeker. If you're stroking any other cows, Jessie will come and headbutt them out of the way because she wants to be stroked! And there was also Jelly Tot, who used to put her head on your shoulder so you could stroke her. At this point, her eyes would roll back because she loved it so much.

Life has changed so much for me since I started coming to the farm. I had no discipline as a child and teenager. My dad was too busy on drugs to even notice, so there were no boundaries. As a teenage girl, I'd be allowed out until whatever time I wanted. To stay over at anyone's house. But when I came in here, they gave me boundaries. It wasn't strict discipline, but there was a line there, one I knew I couldn't cross. You can't be rude, or swear here. At school, you'd be disciplined and end up in detention or isolation. But at the farm, they'd sit me down and explain how I couldn't be speaking like that, but it was a gentle conversation, not an adult just telling me off.

I feel like that's where a lot of schools fail nowadays. Social services too. I think that had I been fostered, things would have gone better for me. I would have gone to school washed and in clean clothes, and having had breakfast. There would have been regular meals, a Christmas I could have looked forward to. But instead, I was at home, raising my little sister, when I was just a child myself.

If the school had been listening or looking properly, they would have seen that I wasn't just a naughty kid. To them, I was a child who had no respect, a troublesome, swearing teen. But in reality, I was getting no love, structure or stability at home. But the truth was, they didn't want me in their school anymore, so I got kicked out. It was as simple as that.

With them and with social services, I wish they had looked beyond the surface.

There were a lot of clues there. I was dirty, not wearing the right clothes to school. I was skinny, malnourished.

Today, I live by myself, and I work as a barmaid. I keep in contact with the farm and I'm doing some courses here. It's my driving theory test at the moment, which is so important to me. They know I never had a meaningful mum or a dad or home life, so even at 20 years old, I need that sort of guidance and stability. Darren's helped me with my theory like a dad would with his daughter. And Sonya is like a second mother. Well, more like my first mother! She and Julie are such great people.

It's been eight years since I first walked through the doors at the farm and I'm still coming in. I feel so close to everyone. Obviously, there are kids who have come and gone, but I know Julie stays in contact with them.

Every single child—no matter what their issue is, no matter how big or small that issue is—has mattered. Julie has loved them almost like her own. Me, Jordan, Reece, who sadly died. You can see the love that she has for all of us.

If school and social services had only listened to me through my actions, they would have understood how horrible things were for me and taken me into care sooner.

I dedicate this story to my son, who keeps me trying to build a better life for him and me.

Panda – tester of bravery. Giving confidence and a topic of social stories.

LIFE ON THE FARM

Showcasing some of our amazing young people – nurturing new skills, cultivating confidence, growing self-esteem and harvesting resilience in an agricultural environment.

Ebeneezer – enjoying fodder beet and being cared for by the young people. Making memories of acceptance.

Mutty – Future Roots Meet and Greet Official.

Misty – always listens.

Alice – being patient to allow a young person to learn new skills.

Harry – soothing and calming, and lowering heart rates.

Preparing animal feed and gaining animal knowledge.

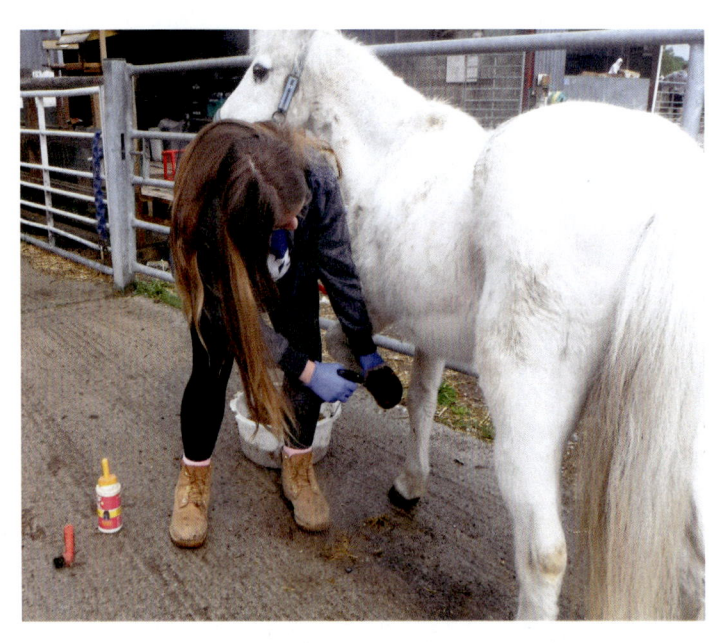

Alice – having her hooves picked out and oiled. Learning skills for future career opportunities.

Mutty – enjoying a belly tickle and encouraging young people to show their feelings.

Nat King Cole – making friends, giving confidence and a feeling of being accepted.

Learning new skills and feeling useful. Boosting self confidence and growing a sense of hope for the future.

Star – forging friendships and the subject of many social stories.

Chicken Licken – showing trust and teaching patience.

Star – having a hug and being patient to allow self soothing.

Julianna – listening to all and hearing everything. Stoic and calm, encouraging young people to mirror behaviours.

Pancake making with a sense of humour. Creating a sense of belonging.

CHAPTER 5: JORDAN'S STORY

My name's Jordan, and I'm 22 years old. I grew up in a home filled with shouting and arguing. My mum and stepdad were always having a go at each other, and I had lots of siblings, so it never felt like a peaceful or stable place.

School wasn't much better. I hated sitting in a classroom for hours on end learning about stuff that didn't feel useful when I could have been working. And I really struggled to concentrate on what the teachers were saying. I've never been tested for dyslexia, but I reckon I have it. So yeah, I hated school and the teachers, and as a result, I was a real pain in the ass.

With such little peace at home and school, I used to hang out in the evenings in the local bus shelter, and before long I was spending time with the wrong crowd. For a while, my life hung in the balance. The people I was with dealt drugs and while it was risky and dangerous, the money came so easily. I got sucked into that lifestyle and let's just say I came close to prison time. But then my life changed.

There were some kids from my school who'd already attended Future Roots at Rylands Farm, and someone must have suggested it could work for me too. I was in Year 9 when I started here. I was a bit iffy about the place at first. To be honest, I wanted to be a mechanic—to follow in my dad's footsteps, even though he wasn't around as I was growing up—so I wasn't convinced that working with animals was going to help much. But it was mostly because I didn't know what to expect, and the unknown can be frightening.

Once I started working with the animals and learning more about what it takes to run a farm, I decided I wanted to do this more than being a mechanic. I could see the scope and potential, I suppose. If you're a mechanic, you're stuck in a garage, whereas a farmer is doing all sorts, including mechanical work and driving machinery.

I didn't talk much at the start, but as I began to get used to the people around me, I opened up more. I didn't trust anyone, but bit by bit, I realised that the staff and other kids weren't out to get me.

I loved driving the tractors obviously, but in time I enjoyed working with the other students and watching them learn new things. The staff were amazing. They were fun and friendly, but also able to listen to me, without any judgement

Most importantly, this place helped to put me on another path. I was still tempted by the easy money I'd been making, and Julie taught me that I could make a living in the right way, without having to look over my shoulder all the time. It would be hard, but it was the right choice. She helped me to believe in myself—that I could be a bigger and better person than the one I thought I was. In time, I went from one day to five days, studying and passing an apprenticeship.

After I left here aged 19, I began to work on a dairy farm. I discovered there was much less variety than I'd hoped for, and it was a bit of a shock. The farmer was very different to the staff here. Much more abrupt, and always ordering me around.

The next farm, run by a man called Richard, was much better. He employed really nice people, but they were pushing me to do a lot of paperwork, which I was maybe not ready to tackle. But I was also impatient and moved on to another farm, where a mate worked.

I now work in a fibreglass factory in Sherborne—a very different environment. It's weird. I've gone from a very physical role, where I was moving around all day long and working with animals, to an indoor job where I sit for eight hours. But I get paid twice as much, and really feel valued.

So yes, I'm not working on a dairy farm, but life is good. I live with my girlfriend's family, who've offered me more love and security than my own ever did.

Looking back, I wish my parents had been able to offer me more security—that they hadn't been arguing so much. I wish they could have spent a bit more time listening to what was going on for me, but they were too caught up in their own lives.

If I had been listened to at primary school, you would have known that life was difficult and I didn't feel able to talk very much. You would have known that I used to get picked on because I couldn't do the work. I had no confidence because I was afraid of trying in case I failed—I would have liked to have been valued for sport.

I dedicate this story to Future Roots, who listened and gave me a chance, and to all young people like me who are struggling like I was.

Alice – teaching patience and understanding.

CHAPTER 6: CHLOE'S STORY

My name's Chloe and I'm 17 years old. I think I was born with a love of animals and the countryside in my blood. They certainly shaped the direction of my life.

My grandparents had a beef farm and my earliest memories were of visiting them—helping with the calves and zooming around the farm on a battery quad bike. The freedom and space surrounded me like a comforting and addictive hug. I remember wishing it would never change.

The cows made me feel calm and safe. They were dependable, which in turn helped me to trust them and I knew they would look after me. I was around five when I begged to be allowed to start showing cows just like my big sister and the rest of my family. I was a force to be reckoned with, often described as 'bossy' by some, but I prefer to think of it as confident.

My dad tried to encourage me to think about doing gymnastics or something else as a hobby because he wanted me to have choices, and not be pressured into showing the cows. But after several heart-to-hearts, he gave in and we got my first Jersey calf. Dad had always shown Holsteins but he thought the smaller-sized Jersey cow would be easier for me to handle, and that I'd be able to show it for longer as I grew older and bigger. I remember I didn't feel at all nervous striding out with my calf around the show ring as a child. I was completely in charge, and I absolutely loved the sensation of winning, the excitement of the competition and the feeling of community and shared interest with my family and fellow competitors, all bound together by their love of cows.

That confidence from the show ring followed me to primary school to start off with, but by the time I was around eight years old, it was obvious to all around me that I was struggling with reading and writing. I went from a bright, vibrant and energetic girl to a shy and nervous one, who felt stupid and thick. From that time on, I was so scared of making mistakes, so I withdrew into myself and kept quiet. My biggest fear was to be asked a question in front of the class that I couldn't answer, so I decided to keep silent. That way, I stayed under the radar and was overlooked. This carried on for another two years until I reached the age of ten.

We moved house that year and I was forced to change schools. Within the first week at my new school, they discovered that I was dyslexic. Support and strategies were soon in place for me. That was a comfort, but I couldn't move beyond the quietness and shyness. The damage was already done and it followed me through all of my future schooling. I was never going to risk being called stupid again.

November 6th 2021 is engrained in my brain for the rest of my life. It started off as a fairly normal day. Dad and I worked together to milk the cows on the farm. We laughed and joked, and danced to the songs on the radio in the parlour as we often did. He was my hero, my god and often my confidant who I could talk to about anything. We revelled in our special time together with the cows—chatting, joking and getting excited about the fireworks display we were going to later on that evening. After milking was finished, we headed out to get some shopping and extra special food for our show cows. We always gave them a little bit more and Dad and I loved treating them.

'Great minds think alike,' he used to say.

Later in the day, we started the second milking of the day. Dad said he felt unwell. I got him a drink of water and he sat down for a while as I carried on with the milking. Halfway through, Dad stood up and immediately collapsed, falling face-first onto the concrete parlour floor. I ran to him and turned him over. He had blood coming out of his mouth and he didn't have a pulse. Panic consumed me. An absolutely overwhelming and terrifying panic.

I rushed to start CPR on him, wiping away the blood and after a couple of minutes, I grabbed my phone to call Mum for help. She arrived soon after and I went outside to wait for the ambulance. I was shaking uncontrollably from the shock and disbelief of what was happening. After the ambulance arrived, it turned to devastation and a kind of numbness, as the crew said they didn't think Dad was going to make it.

My dad died that day. Never for a single moment did I think that I would ever have to say goodbye to him in the dairy surrounded by his adoring cows. It just wasn't right. He was way too young to go and leave me. We had so many more trips to make to the beach, the speedway and the greyhound racing track we used to visit together.

ARE YOU LISTENING NOW?

My shock quickly turned to anger when I discovered that people from the village had heard the ambulance and met it at the farm gate to see what was going on, even trying to film it on their phones. Thankfully the ambulance crew spoke with them before my anger surfaced outwardly. After Dad was taken away, I had to call my brother and sister and explain what had happened. For us all, it became the worst day of our lives, after which, nothing would ever be the same again.

I walked back onto the farmyard to see Adam, one of the farm workers on his knees, crying in the parlour at the loss of his friend. He had to finish the milking that we had started hours ago. My heart broke for him and for us!

Later that evening I sat in silence and listened to the popping and cracking of the fireworks in the background. The very same fireworks that just that morning we had been so excited to go and see. Now I couldn't even look at them, and I still can't to this day.

Over the next few days, the awkwardness set in and people avoided us as they didn't know what to say. A feeling of isolation came over me and all I felt that I had left now were the fond memories of better times with my dad. I was allowed two weeks off from school, but it didn't feel long enough. I asked for help in the form of counselling but was told there was no space for me. It made me feel like I didn't matter because others were receiving it. Again I felt overlooked and it just made me shrink back into myself even more at school. The one day a week I did look forward to was Thursday. This was the day that I got to go to Future Roots at Rylands Farm. This was my saviour day. It got me away from school and I felt listened to there. The staff would help support me and let me talk about my dad. They remembered things, important things to me that mattered. They understood me.

It's now been two years since Dad died. I want to be brave and help other young people who have had a bereavement in their family to understand that they are not alone; I want to reach out to them to say please talk to someone about how you're feeling, and don't bottle it up. If you're worried about upsetting your family by doing this, try to talk to someone unconnected, like a trusted teacher or even a counsellor. It definitely worked for me and now two years on, I am able to look back at my amazing dad with the best memories—ones that help to make me smile every time I recall them. I truly had the best dad, even though it was for a shorter time.

I am working hard at agricultural college now to make him proud of me and in turn, it's helping me to get back to the carefree, confident, Chloe that I was when I was a young girl.

I want to send a message to schools and those that have the power to change things for young people, that if schools had listened to me they would known that being withdrawn is not in my nature and just because I was quiet it didn't mean that I was coping with my loss. I asked for counselling and I had never asked for anything before. I felt let down.

I want to dedicate this story to Dad, who gave me the building blocks to create my future life and the love of cows. There is not a day that goes by when I don't think of him. He will always be with me in my heart.

Champion show cow giving confidence and building self esteem.

CHAPTER 7: VEE'S STORY

My name's Vee, and I'm 17 years old. I was an easy, happy baby who grew into a little girl who liked her food, particularly chicken chow mein, apparently! One of my earliest memories was when I was five and staying at a holiday cottage. It was there that I saw snow for the first time, and built a snowman.

Despite these happy moments, there was a lot of sadness in my childhood. My dad left when I was three months old and didn't return until I was five. Even then, he didn't stay long. I recently found out that for all those years, Mum sent cards and presents to me pretending that they were from him. Discovering that really hurt. Mum had tried her best to make me feel that Dad still cared, so I don't blame her, but I do feel resentment towards Dad for just evaporating, and never caring.

We then went through a really rough period when Mum was struggling with addictions. Eventually, we became homeless, moving from one of her partners to the next. It was a horrible time. In total, there were seven different partners and only one was nice. The rest were threatening, aggressive addicts. I was scared so much of the time.

When I was eight years old, I moved in with my grandparents, who by then had legal guardianship of me. Mum was pregnant again and there was going to be no room for me in the place where we lived. I felt pushed out and rejected by her, and that made me really sad. Why did I have to move and not any of the others? I was at least safe at Gran and Granddad's, although I was too upset to properly appreciate it at the time.

My grandparents were lovely people but very old school, the type who didn't hug. There was such a generation gap between us. I remember going bra shopping aged 11 with Grandad and feeling incredibly awkward. He didn't really know how to do that sort of stuff.

Fortunately, I enjoyed school, where I loved the attention and did my best to be top of the class. I wanted not only to be liked by others but to win my grandparents' favour. I always wanted to be the best at everything I could.

Everything changed when I reached nine years old. I had made some good friends and would often go to my best friend's house after school for tea. Her older brother appeared to be very interested in me, and after a while, he told me that he wanted to walk me to the bus stop. He said he wanted to keep me 'safe.' It never struck me as strange that he was walking me and not his own sister. I was only nine—I thought he loved me and that I loved him too. But that year, after grooming me for weeks, he sexually assaulted me. I wish it was an isolated incident but the truth is, this horrifying ordeal continued until I was 12 years old.

I didn't speak about it until I was 15 years old. I just didn't know how to. The only way I could show that something was wrong was by being very angry and rebellious—smoking, drinking and taking drugs. I said some awful things to my grandparents at that time but I was hurting so much that I didn't care.

Eventually, I was taken into foster care. The first placement didn't work out. I'd been there for a year when it broke down, and I returned to Gran's house. Grandad had died when I was 14 years old, so it was just me and Gran by this point. She was a huge support and did her very best to keep me on the straight and narrow, but my old demons had returned and things took a downward plunge. I started getting into alcohol and drugs, and poor Gran didn't really know how to deal with it. She was already grieving the loss of Grandad and I think she decided to turn a blind eye to my bad habits as she was afraid of losing me as well, which she maybe feared might happen if she cracked down on me. I was soon in such a bad place. I just couldn't see any future for myself and ended up self-harming and taking a series of overdoses.

I was soon back in foster care again, but this time in a residential care home rather than a family home. It could have got even worse for me, but it was at this time that I also started at Future Roots at Rylands Farm. It was here that I studied for my Functional Skills (English and Maths), but also finally began looking forward in a more hopeful way. The mentors helped me to better understand my needs and to find the motivation to plan for the future. I joined college to continue my English and Maths and also took some vocational units in employability. This brings me to the present day when, at the time of writing, I'm about to take my GCSEs.

ARE YOU LISTENING NOW?

I'm 17 years old now and still in foster care, but I'm looking to the future with so much more hope and positivity. I'm in a stable relationship and hoping to move into a home with my partner next year when I'm 18 years old. I also plan to study a psychology course and embark on a nursing apprenticeship so in time I can help other young people who, like me, have had challenges in their lives.

I want to take this opportunity to say how important it is you focus on being yourself. Don't feel like you need to change yourself so others will like you.

I just feel that if you had listened to me growing up you would have heard that I was unhappy and felt different to others. I really just wanted to be wanted.

I would like to dedicate my story to two people. The first is a very special social worker called Jade, who was with me for three years. She listened when I needed it the most, and that meant so much to me. The second person is my current partner Connor, who has seen me at my worst and still stuck with me. I can't tell you how good that feels. Here's to a happy future!

Self expression. Knowing who you are.

CHAPTER 8: ABI'S STORY

My name's Abi, and I'm 29 years old. From what I've been told, I was an easy, happy baby. My earliest memory is from when I was six years old, and I was bitten by a friend's German Shepherd. Instead of taking me to a doctor or hospital, my mother treated the wound with TCP, which stung so much. It's probably why the memory is so strong!

Around that time, I began to realise my life was very different to my friends. My dad was an alcoholic and he and my mum often argued, which frightened me and made me feel insecure, and there was quite a lot of chaos in the house. I envied my friends' happy home lives and their lunchboxes which, unlike mine, were full of nice things. I didn't enjoy school. I can't explain why, but it felt so claustrophobic being confined inside those four walls. But at the same time, I didn't want to be at home either.

In time, my father's alcoholism began to have an effect on family life. He was a lorry driver, and after a drink-driving incident, he lost his license and couldn't work. That put a strain on the family finances and led to even more frequent and heated arguments. Dad was aggressive when drunk. Despite being a daddy's girl when he was sober, I felt scared and unsafe around him when he was intoxicated. Soon after, my mother fell into depression, and their marriage eventually ended.

To escape the scary, heated atmosphere at home, I used to seek refuge at a neighbour's house. She was kind and understanding. I never revealed the details of my family situation to her, although she probably had an idea that things weren't right. I did confide in my Year 3 teacher about my parents' split, but I got in trouble for it, which made me more guarded about sharing personal stuff with anyone else.

My school attendance suffered, and the messy state of our home reflected the chaos in my life. School would send someone to pick me up in the mornings to help. While Mum could function just about well enough to go to work, she couldn't cope with running a home, which was a total tip. By secondary school, I was choosing to be at friends' homes, often avoiding being at home altogether. I struggled academically, especially in maths, and despite a five-month absence from school, I received little in the way of extra support and couldn't catch up. Unsurprisingly, around this time, I turned to smoking and drinking, which helped distract me from my life and problems.

At 13, I started coming to Future Roots at Rylands Farm. I didn't realise it at the time, but it was the beginning of a better period. The farm was a place where I almost instantly felt more comfortable. It probably sounds strange, but I was able to express myself by talking to the animals. After a while, I realised the mentors weren't going to judge me, and I started to open up to them. For the first time in a very long while, I felt heard and began to experience the first stirrings of hope.

ARE YOU LISTENING NOW?

With my confidence growing, I found a job working for a woman in my village who had horses. I would help her care for the animals and in return, she gave me riding lessons. This brought me a focus and some structure during daylight hours, but after dark, it was another story. I still craved something to keep me out of the house, and I would meet up with older boys I didn't know and go for joyrides at high speed in their cars. I was only 15 years old, but it was the distraction I needed, an adrenaline rush that helped me forget. I felt as if nobody cared, so I just carried on doing it, living in the moment.

Some nights, I would lie on an upturned boat in our local park and stare at the stars, dreaming of a better future—nice man, nice job, nice home and happy kids—but I really didn't think I would ever get to enjoy those things.

About this time, I made a friend called Lucy at the farm. She would often wait up until the early hours of the morning to check that I got home safe. At first, I wasn't sure what to make of her. Nobody had cared in the past—why would she?

At 16, I enrolled in an equine course at a nearby college. I did really well academically, becoming the top student in my year, which felt like such an achievement given my life so far, and how broken my education had been.

But after college, my life soon began to unravel. I had a series of shallow relationships and just as many jobs. Most of them were tied to a relationship, so when one finished, the other did too. In between, I would return to my mum's house, but I felt she was more of a landlord than a parent. It was transactional rather than loving.

It was during one of these times of being at my mum's that I found work in the care industry. It proved to be a turning point for me. I loved the attention that I received from the clients, and felt like I was giving something back to them besides the care. I was often the only person who they had seen that day, so my company meant a lot to them. I eventually got a healthcare assistant job in a hospital and loved training in all of the different departments, discovering how a hospital operated and what the specialities were. To me, this felt like learning with a purpose, which made me feel engaged and focused.

I finally settled on a career in the emergency department, where every day presents new challenges. I love it!

During a shift at the hospital, I met a policeman who had often tried to reach out to me during my difficult teenage years. I'd totally forgotten that I had written him a letter, telling him how much better things were now. But he hadn't, and he'd then taken the time to come say hello, and say two words that meant the world to me—'well done.' His kindness that day felt like a validation of everything I'd achieved against all the odds. I'd overcome so much, and he saw that.

Life has since brought me to a place of stability, with a rewarding career, two wonderful children, and a supportive partner. I share my story as proof that you can overcome obstacles, and to encourage others facing similar challenges to seek help and support.

If you had been listening to me at primary school, you would have heard that I wanted to learn, but I didn't feel safe so concentrating in class was really difficult. I just wanted you to understand.

I dedicate this story to myself, acknowledging the hurdles I've overcome, and to anyone who can relate, reminding them that help is available if they are brave enough to ask for it.

Blossom tree – it marks spring, growth, warmth and happiness ahead.

CONCLUSION

By Yvonne Shell: Associate Professor in Forensic Psychology, Registered Clinical and Forensic Psychologist, CPsychol, CSci, AFBPsS

Introduction

Consistent themes across the chapters included in this book speak of sadness, disappointment, fear and frustration, at the experience of not being seen, heard and listened to, at critical moments in individual lives, and in relation to critical events. Amongst these pages, Lucy, Charlie and Reece, all testify to this experience:

'I wish school had listened to me about the bullying.'
'If the school had been listening and looking properly…'
'I wish they had looked beyond the surface…'
'They thought what I said was real… I didn't mean what I said, but no one really listened… If I said something, they wouldn't bother to find out what was true and what was just an act.'

Whilst the contributors to this book report diverse background narratives, there are common threads running through each lived experience of childhood and adolescence, eg, being a 'looked after' child by a local authority, disrupted education, school exclusion, school bullying, involvement in crime, caring responsibilities within the family home, exposure to family addiction, domestic violence and involvement in gang culture. Consequently, the stories included here can be positioned as being offered by marginalised youth, often with complex learning needs.

The accounts report on experiences of negative power being exerted upon the individual by professionals involved in their care, resulting in feelings of being unseen, unheard and misunderstood. This in turn giving rise to feelings of increased threat and exclusion from positive peer groups, community and society more widely. They tell the reader that being a child in care or marginalised in any way, silences the person. Silencing is a complex phenomenon, it can be both intentional and unintentional, and it can occur through self-silencing, (eg, through fear or shame about the experiences a child has lived through) or silencing from the listener when accounts are not believed, and through poor and insensitive listening and management around the child.

What is apparent in these pages is that mainstream education was not meeting the needs of these young people, and yet the alternative educational/vocational provisions were often negatively positioned, for example, a 'school for misfits' as described by one young person in this book. Asking young people to attend vocational education that is held in lower esteem than mainstream academic education, places this group firmly within a deficit mode, with discourses of underachievement underpinning them. This may serve to further mute the voices of these young people, whereby stereotypes of marginalised children and youth, effectively justifies their alienation and removal from the mainstream, and in doing so contributes to decreasing and nullifying their voices.

Not Listening Then

Not being listened to, results in feelings of being devalued and to subsequent feelings of powerlessness. Not listening is more than not hearing, it is effectively 'silencing' the speaker. Having your voice listened to and heard, means you and your life experiences matter, and this is paramount to an individual's psychological well-being, and in the formation of a healthy identity. Truly listening to the voice of young people confers dignity and respect to the speaker to engage with curiosity and openness to listening, whilst adopting positive and trustworthy intent as a listener, is critical in this process.

Professionals not asking the right questions, not demonstrating enough curiosity to explore what is being said at depth, were also reported. It is no surprise that this in turn may result in feelings of learned helplessness on the part of the young person, who then may engage in self-silencing, replete with moral emotions of shame and blame, believing they are indeed just 'bad people' who do 'bad things.' We must also guard against the paradoxical effect of when some voices are experienced as loud, they can be further vilified and marginalised. It is a fact that some children are demonised and subject to intensified scrutiny and regulation often to make service providers feel 'safe,' rather than in service to trying to make the child feel 'safe.' A belief by the young person that services/professionals will not help may drive them closer to belonging elsewhere, this 'elsewhere' may be 'risky' and lead to a reinforcement of the trope that they are 'bad.' You can see evidence for this in Reece's story within this book.

A variety of contextual and contingent factors make the process of help-seeking by young people a complex one. It is the responsibility of the professional to understand and listen to how young people perceive those charged with their care, and consider how each young person views the availability and accessibility of professionals in services. If young people anticipate that a problem cannot be resolved or may possibly be made worse by contact with professionals, then the result is a fundamental breakdown in trust that prevents useful dialogue and support.

The movement to hear the lived experiences of groups of people, to aid in understanding the experiences of those individuals and to shape policy and practice, has been gaining momentum slowly, as evidenced for example by the #MeToo movement. It is, however, too slow in coming to the voices of children and young people.

Why Don't We Listen? Implications for Practice

One reason we may not as a society listen to children is that we live in a culture in which Childism exists, even if inadvertently. Childism has been referred to by Wall (2019, 2021) as 'a pervasive and profound, cultural hostility towards children, deeply embedded in social structures of domination and in state apparatuses of exploitation and subordination.' The negative element of Childism speaks to power relations, oppressive dynamics, and results in discrimination and marginalisation of children, removing agency and voice from the child. We need to combat the scepticism and myths around children and young people about not having a voice equal to that of an adult. We must also consider that if Childism is present for all children, how much more so for marginalised children.

By reading this book you are demonstrating the courage to listen to the voices of each contributor here. Not listening to a young person's narrative can be construed in and of itself as a trauma for the young person, compounding the life experiences that have brought that young person under the remit of services. There is recognition of the 'redemptive quality of empowering narration' of a person with lived experience that is acknowledged in the literature base by Delker *et al* (2021), as cited in Brown, Shell and Cole (2023).

Furthermore, it is not possible to respond helpfully if we are not wholeheartedly curious about understanding the lived experience of the young person. To do this we have to ask the right questions, this demands that we are interested and listen, remaining present and engaged in the process, demonstrating that we can tolerate the enormity of what is being communicated to us. This process takes time, and we are in a moment of significant under-resourcing and unprecedented demand on professionals in services. This should alert us to the fact that every contact we make with a young person is critical and that we must make every contact matter. However, when demand is high and professionals feel under significant pressure, it is human nature to respond with a 'fixed mindset,' the use of cognitive bias, thinking shortcuts (heuristics), become more prevalent and we operate from a narrow, threat-based position, removing the opportunity for creativity and compassion. This chapter urges professionals to 'notice' this, and in noticing to make the conscious decision to change this in their own practice.

We need to compassionately ask the question, 'What do I/we need to ask you to find out about your life, what's happened to you, and what is important to you?' Rather than seeking evidence to answer the question, 'What's wrong with you?'

Secondary trauma and vicarious trauma for professionals hearing these accounts is a risk and our response to this should not be self-protection through avoidance of listening, but rather through staff training, supervision and reflective practice.

This book is vitally important as we have a moral responsibility to engage justly with young people. Crucial conversations need to be done with care and as mentioned earlier, every contact matters. The use of voice does not simply and routinely result in empowerment, as voice has to 'land' and resonate with the listener. To leave the responsibility to the young participants to get their voices heard is ethically and morally unsound. When we listen to the voices of the young people who have contributed here, we need to respect their narratives whilst also situating them within a social and historical context. None of these accounts occur in a vacuum.

Strikingly, all the participants in this book remained determined to have their voices listened to. One hopes that this opportunity to record their narratives will offer a healing experience for each, although, for one contributor, Reece, this intervention comes too late. For the remaining contributors, we hope that this book may mark the beginning of the process of repair for earlier histories of repeated silencing and invalidation. Many here report on how finding a safe and secure place at Rylands Farm, where they experienced a strong sense of acceptance and belonging, where they were listened to in a non-judgmental way, was fundamental to their wellbeing. This in turn facilitated the development of self-belief and self-confidence, paramount to young people subsequently achieving occupational aspirations, becoming purposeful contributors to their communities and to society more widely. Perhaps part of the experience at Rylands Farm also contributed to the young persons' continued determination to have their voices listened to now. Professionals need to engage with the powerful motive of compassion with this group of children. Compassion is one of our most courageous of human motives. Every one of the contributors in this book is our future, and our ability to listen to their narratives without blaming, or avoiding their reality is paramount. When are we going to be as courageous as the young contributors here? This book is a challenge to us all, there are no observers to the care of children and young people in this country, we are all in this.

I leave you with the powerful words of Reece, a young man who died whilst 'under' the care of services, and whose wisdom in this sentiment expressed below should ring in your ears as you finish this book:

'If you had been listening, you would have heard.'

Our challenge is to listen now.

EPILOGUE: HARVESTING HOPE

This book has been lottery-funded to help young people share their lives to benefit others. The stories show what makes a difference—it's not theory or solving every problem. It's about being present and giving time to listen.

There is always a good reason why Future Roots is needed for the young people who attend. For many starting with life circumstances that are out of the young people's control. Exacerbated by challenging events that continually happen to some, or one-off traumatic events that impact at critical times in young people's lives. We know the impact Covid had on many people, creating anxiety and isolation.

As a result of traumatic individual events or long-term sustained challenges, some young people go into flight, fright or freeze mode whenever they are faced with fear, frustration or emotional situations. The behaviours can then be misread and tough to manage in public settings or institutions where there is a narrow expectation of what is acceptable. At these times, young people need to be really listened to—words can be misconstrued; a show of emotion judged as a risk. It takes the right person and the right environment, and even with that, it needs to be the right time for the young person to be able to say what they want to say.

ARE YOU LISTENING NOW?

In 18 years at Future Roots and 25 years as a social worker, I have not met a young person who doesn't want to be valued or a young person who doesn't want to learn. When life is really tough and it feels like you have no choice, control or voice, we have heard the importance of feeling heard.

I would like to dedicate the Future Roots Journey to all the young people who have taught us so much and reinforced our belief that we shouldn't stop listening and we should never give up on them.

Julie Plumley

Mutty – helping young people to feel safe and express feelings.

StoryTerrace